Anne
Boleyn

Valerie Shrimplin

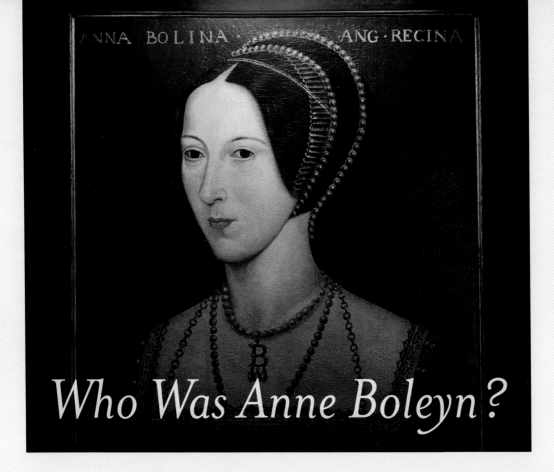

ANNA BOLINA · ANG · RECINA

Who Was Anne Boleyn?

Anne Boleyn – a scheming, ambitious temptress, or the highly educated mother of one of England's greatest rulers? Far more is known about Anne's fate and her execution on 19 May 1536 than about her life, appearance and character.

There are many unanswered questions about Anne's short life. What was her precise date of birth? Did she really keep Henry VIII waiting for six years before sharing his bed? Were they in love or did they both just lust for power? Can Anne Boleyn be regarded as one of the most forward-thinking of English queens, with a passion for reform and 'the new learning'? Or was she only interested in having a good time, enjoying court life and the riches it brought her?

Henry VIII's fears for the Tudor dynasty and his endless quest for a male heir characterised his reign; but the course of history can easily turn and change. What if Henry's elder brother, Prince Arthur, had lived? Or if Henry's first wife, Catherine of Aragon, had given birth to a healthy son? What if Anne Boleyn had herself produced a male heir, instead of her daughter Elizabeth? Henry was not to know that this daughter would put paid to all the arguments that a female monarch would be a disaster.

Anne Boleyn's story is one of the great dramas of the 16th century – a classic tale of love, death and money.

Family Background

ABOVE: This Hans Holbein the Younger portrait of Anne's father, Thomas Boleyn, has also been identified as James Butler, Earl of Ormond.

INSET: Elizabeth Boleyn, Anne's mother.

Anne Boleyn is sometimes described as something of an 'upstart', descended from the merchant Boleyn (or 'Bullen') family, although her father, Sir Thomas Boleyn, had some noble blood and owned Blickling Hall in Norfolk and Hever Castle in Kent. He married into the wealthy and powerful Howard family; his wife, Elizabeth, was the daughter of the Duke of Norfolk. They had several children of whom Mary, Anne and George survived to adulthood.

Sir Thomas rose swiftly as an ambitious politician and diplomat, becoming Treasurer of the Royal Household and Lord Privy Seal. In later life he also became Earl of Wiltshire, Earl of Ormond and Viscount Rochford.

His daughter Anne was probably born at the family's Norfolk estate, Blickling Hall, but her precise date of birth is unknown. Her age is significant when considering whether she was a mature woman or a young girl when she became involved with King Henry, and whether she was well into her 30s or much younger when she died. Until recently her year of birth was generally given as 1507 because contemporaries noted that she was particularly young when she went overseas and 'not 29 years old' when executed. The year 1501 is now argued as more probable, due to the existence of a letter from Anne to her father around 1514, which could not have been written by a very young person.

Early Years

As a young girl in 1513, Anne Boleyn was sent to be a maid of honour at the court of Margaret of Austria, regent of the Netherlands, where Anne's father had been ambassador. Margaret's court was effectively an exclusive international 'finishing school' for aristocratic young ladies and, as well as being exposed to courtly behaviour and chivalry, Anne would have been well-educated.

"I find her so bright and pleasant for her young age that I am more beholden to you for sending her to me than you are to me."

ARCHDUCHESS MARGARET OF AUSTRIA TO SIR THOMAS BOLEYN

The French royal court

Anne left the Netherlands for Paris in 1514, joining the sophisticated and stylish household of Queen Claude, wife of Francis I, in 1515. As well as becoming fluent in French, and developing her interests in humanist thought and 'the new learning', Anne would also have been further immersed in chivalric ideas of courtly love, involving the latest fashions and etiquette, along with music, singing and dancing. Naturally vivacious, she would have learned how to use her charms and courtly graces in order to attract the interest of admirers and potential husbands.

Return to England

England's relations with France deteriorated, and in 1522 Anne was recalled home for an arranged marriage to her cousin James Butler, heir to the Earl of Ormond. The marriage did not proceed so Anne joined the household of Henry VIII's wife, Queen Catherine of Aragon, as lady-in-waiting. She soon became noticed, particularly for her beautiful eyes, as she joined in the festivities and dancing at the royal court.

A lavish entertainment in 1522 at York Place in Westminster, Cardinal Thomas Wolsey's episcopal palace, seems to be the mostly likely occasion of Anne's first meeting with Henry VIII, even though his serious romancing of her probably did not begin in earnest until about 1525.

Meanwhile, Anne was pursued by several courtly gentlemen, specifically the poet Thomas Wyatt and Henry Percy, son and heir of the Earl of Northumberland, with whom she fell in love and was even possibly secretly betrothed in 1523.

RIGHT: Portrait of Archduchess Margaret of Austria by Bernard van Orley.

BELOW: Queen Claude, wife of Francis I. Anne spent seven years at the French Court, serving Queen Claude.

Did you know?

Anne's years at the court of Queen Claude completely imbued her with French culture and education, causing French diplomat Lancelot de Carles to remark, 'No one would ever have taken her to be English by her manners, but a native-born French woman.'

5

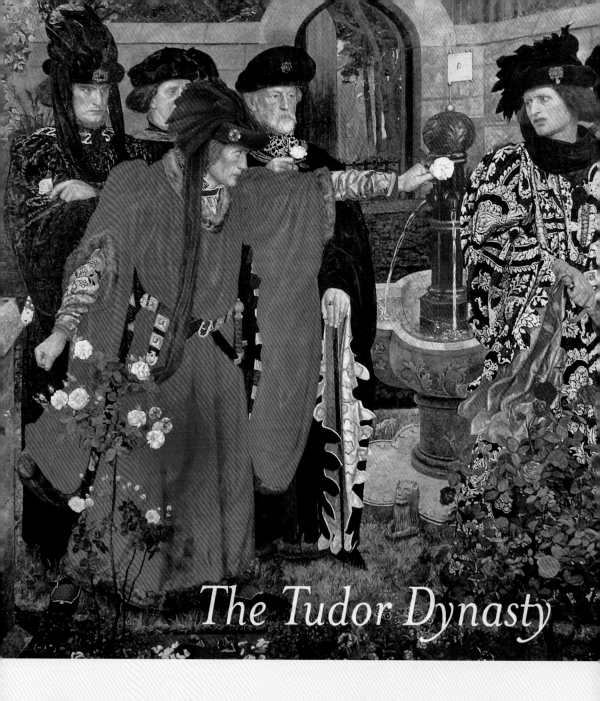

The Tudor Dynasty

I t is impossible to understand the Tudors without appreciating the dynastic struggles of the Wars of the Roses between the Houses of York and Lancaster which had torn the country apart since the 1450s. Henry VIII's father, Henry VII, had a somewhat shaky claim to the throne, founding the Tudor dynasty when he defeated the Yorkist King Richard III at the Battle of Bosworth Field in 1485.

Henry VII's marriage to the Yorkist Princess Elizabeth in 1486 helped stabilise the situation, as did the betrothal of their eldest son, Prince Arthur,

ABOVE: *Plucking the Red and White Roses in the Old Temple Gardens*, by Henry Payne, 1908.

to the Spanish heiress Catherine of Aragon, which gained them powerful allies abroad. The marriage ceremony took place in 1501 but within six months 15-year-old Arthur was dead.

A new king

After his father died in 1509, the 17-year-old King Henry VIII determined to ensure the continued success of the Tudor dynasty. Wishing to retain the alliance – and dowry – and daunted by what now rested on his shoulders, one of Henry's first acts as sovereign was to marry his brother's 25-year-old widow. Catherine soon fell pregnant; she miscarried a girl in 1510 but gave birth to an eagerly anticipated son in 1511. The baby lived less than two months, however, and these early tragedies were followed by four further miscarriages and still-born babies. Only Mary, born in 1516, survived to adulthood, but a female heir was considered impossible since whoever she married would undoubtedly take over the kingdom.

Henry and Catherine's marriage

Henry did, to begin with at least, respect, even love, Catherine. However, the lack of a legitimate male heir must have weighed heavily. An uncertain succession placed the country at real risk of invasion or further civil war. Henry started having extra-marital relationships as early as 1510 and his long-term affair with Bessie Blount c.1514–22 was widely known, since he acknowledged his son by her in 1519, naming him Henry Fitzroy.

By the 1520s, Catherine was losing her looks and becoming a religious fanatic. Henry was very aware of the precarious position of the Tudor dynasty and he took steps to eliminate rivals such as the Duke of Buckingham, with execution being the preferred form of dismissal.

In December 1525, Catherine turned 40. She had experienced seven pregnancies, with only one surviving child. By now, Henry was starting to question the validity of his marriage and why he was not able to have a son. Could it be linked to widely held ideas, based on the scriptures, that there was a connection between divine favour and successful procreation? By this time also, he had noticed a very lively and attractive new member of court: Anne Boleyn.

ABOVE: Portrait of Catherine of Aragon, 18th-century copy of a lost original, by an unknown artist.
LEFT: Henry VIII as a young man when Duke of York.

Love and Passion at the English Court

A nne Boleyn was a stylish and cultivated young lady whose energy and vitality made her the centre of attention. She brought with her to the royal court the latest fashions, such as the French hood – far more attractive and revealing than traditional gabled headgear. Although adept at the game of courtly love, she stopped short of improper liaisons in order to ensure her marriageability. Henry had been having an affair with her older sister, Mary, and Anne had no wish to become another discarded royal mistress.

What did Anne look like?

Portraits and descriptions of Anne were largely produced later, often by people anxious to discredit her. A damaged medallion of 1534 seems to be the only contemporary image of her. Many referred to her beautiful dark eyes but, by contrast, Nicholas Sander,

"Madame Anne is not one of the handsomest women in the world; she is of middling stature, swarthy complexion, long neck, wide mouth, bosom not much raised ... her eyes are black and beautiful."

VENETIAN DIARIST

a Catholic priest opposed to her, later claimed that she had physical deformities including 'a large wen [growth] under her throat' and 'on her right hand, six fingers'. The alleged 'sixth finger' was not mentioned during her lifetime although a later supporter noted there was 'upon the side of her nail upon one of her fingers some little show of a nail which was yet so small'.

Anne and Henry's courtship

It is likely that Anne and Henry's relationship began in 1525. Henry turned 34 that year and was becoming anxious since Catherine was now unlikely to produce a male heir. Did Henry simply need to be free to marry? Or free to marry Anne?

LEFT: A painting from 1835 showing Henry and Anne at royal court.

There is clear evidence that Henry fell deeply in love with the captivating Anne. A courtier observed: 'The long hid and secret love between the king and Mistress Anne Boleyn began to break out into every man's ears.' The king's infatuation with Anne is demonstrated in his letters, of which 17 survive. These provide evidence of his wooing of Anne and her resistance; her gradual acceptance of his advances; and then the hope that they could soon be married.

TOP RIGHT: Anne Boleyn, attributed to John Hoskins.

Early on, Henry promised: 'If it shall please you … to give yourself up, body and soul, to me … I promise you that I will take you for my only mistress.' This was clearly not an offer of marriage. Later, he pined: 'I would you were in mine arms, or I in yours, for I think it long since I kissed you.' The love-sick Henry signed off several letters with a heart shape enclosing their initials, declaring that he sought no other. The pair even exchanged love notes during Mass, scribbled in an illuminated Book of Hours.

LEFT: The Annunciation, from an illuminated Book of Hours, with a handwritten inscription from Anne to Henry: '… you shalle me fynde / to be to you bothe loving and kynde'.

RIGHT: An artist's impression of Anne and Henry at Hever.

A Proposal of Marriage

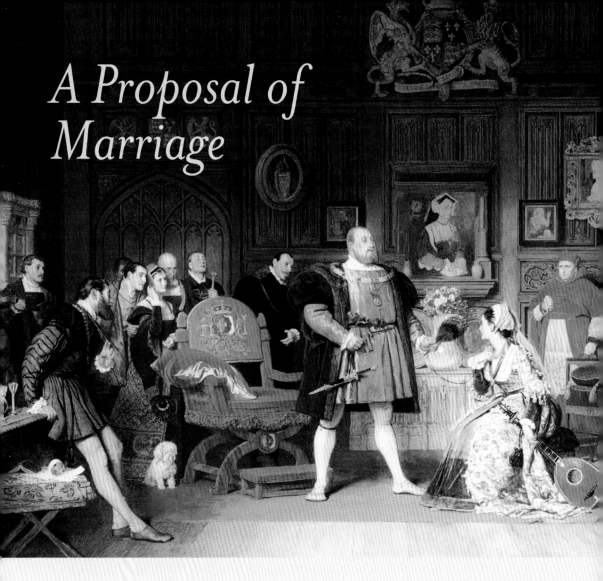

ABOVE: A Victorian
painting showing
Anne and Henry
being observed by
Catherine of Aragon
through an open
door. Her portrait
hangs on the wall
behind them.

Haunted by the biblical reference (Leviticus 20:21) that prohibited a man from marrying his brother's widow, Henry saw God's disapproval as the reason for his lack of a son. 'The King's Great Matter', as it became known, may have originated as a matter of conscience in Henry's wish for a son, but was now inextricably linked with Anne Boleyn.

Henry remained celibate in his relationship with Anne, as confirmed by one of his letters in which he wrote 'henceforth my heart will be devoted to you only, greatly wanting that my body also could be'. Anne declined to become his mistress until the ring was on her finger; and Henry may have been concerned that any child born of the union must be of unquestioned legitimacy. Neither of them was to know the length of time that would be needed for their marriage to be possible, but it was expected to be achieved swiftly and easily.

RIGHT: Portrait of Catherine of Aragon, c.1520.

Anne treated as a queen

Henry proposed to Anne by letter in January 1527. In reply, she sent him a symbolic gift of a jewel depicting a maiden on a storm-tossed ship. After this, they started to appear in public together. He danced with her publicly and she accompanied him on a royal progress. In a curious love-triangle, Anne spent more and more time with Henry at Greenwich Palace while Catherine was still in residence, and he treated the younger woman as queen on State occasions.

Henry seeks an annulment

In June 1527, Cardinal Thomas Wolsey was instructed to open formal proceedings with Rome to investigate the validity of Henry's first marriage, but Catherine refused to co-operate. Besides, Pope Clement VII was currently the prisoner of Catherine's powerful nephew Charles V, King of Spain and Holy Roman Emperor, following the Sack of Rome in May 1527.

Henry's request for an annulment and dispensation to marry another was repeated in 1528, and he was optimistic that matters would soon be resolved.

The investigation, to be heard in front of Cardinal Campeggio at the Legatine Court at Blackfriars, opened on 31 May 1529. Catherine spoke in her own defence, insisting that she was Henry's true wife … then stormed out. The whole process was becoming centred on Henry's growing resolve to reduce the power of the Pope and break with Rome – a massive step since the Roman Catholic Church had been a focus of the traditions and daily way of life in England for more than 1,500 years.

Did you know?

Anne Boleyn nearly died in June 1528 after contracting the terrible 'sweating sickness'. Henry dared not visit her and fervently wished for the recovery of she 'whom I value more than the world'. He was hugely relieved when his beloved Anne returned to health some weeks later.

Breaking with Rome

The Reformation was gaining impetus and Anne drew the new ideas to Henry's attention. William Tyndale's English translation of the New Testament had been published in 1526 and reform writings were circulating at court, particularly the *Supplication for Beggars* by Simon Fish (1528), which protested that the poor were starving because of all the money going to the Church.

ABOVE: *The Trial of Queen Catherine of Aragon* by Baron Henry Nelson O'Neil, 1846–48.

Continued negotiations

Catherine continued to insist she was Henry's true and faithful wife, asserting in November 1529 that, whilst the theologians, academics and lawyers at the universities of Oxford, Cambridge and Paris supported Henry, she could find scholars who would agree with her instead.

In 1530 it was declared that the Pope had no jurisdiction over Henry's marriage. It was a tradition in England that 'no cause having its origin in this country should be advoked to another kingdom' and the King of England was absolute in his own realm. Henry made it clear that if the Pope refused to grant the annulment, he would proceed anyway, with the help and military backing of France.

Wolsey had been unsuccessful in gaining Henry's annulment and, according to the law of *praemunire* (1392), it was an offence to assert the power of any foreign jurisdiction or to take sides with foreign powers against the king. Wolsey was arrested in York in November 1530; he fell ill and died in Leicester on 29 November, on his way back to London to face trial.

The annulment progresses

Henry and Anne spent more and more time together in public, so that people would become used to the idea of her as queen. She increasingly accompanied him on formal occasions, while Catherine was finally moved to Kimbolton Castle, Cambridgeshire on the edge of the Fens – rather like going into a nunnery, which she had refused to do. She never saw Henry again.

The case for the annulment proceeded and Anne, seeing marriage within her grasp, adopted a new livery and motto for Christmas 1530: *'Ainsi sera, groigne qui groigne'* (Thus it will be, grumble who will). The Pope threatened to excommunicate Henry if he married Anne without the Church's permission, whilst the complex negotiations on breaking with Rome and disentangling the country from foreign control continued.

By 1531, progress was made at last. Henry was first declared Supreme Head of the Church in England – with the proviso 'so long as the law of

Christ allows'. The following year, the significant additional clause was removed and a treaty was entered into with France specifying mutual support and defence against the Emperor. In order to prevent others looking to Rome, the *Submission of the Clergy* and the *Act of Annates* (ending massive payments to Rome) were passed in 1532. The unsympathetic Archbishop of Canterbury William Warham died in August 1532, enabling Henry to replace him with the scholar Thomas Cranmer.

LEFT: Thomas Wolsey
by an unknown artist.

Anne's Marriage and Coronation

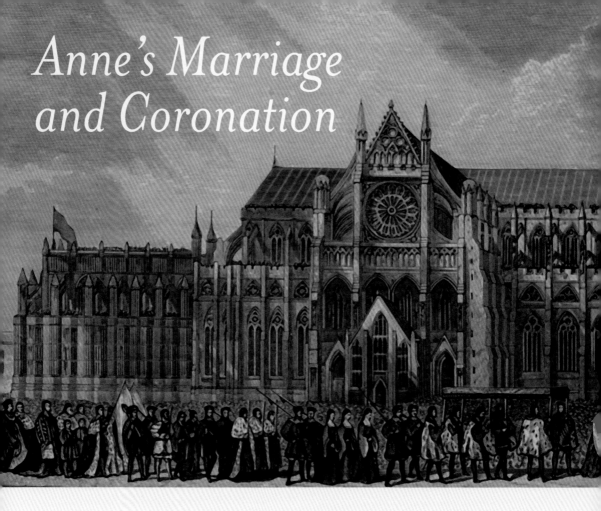

I n 1532 Anne was made Lady Marquis of Pembroke, before accompanying Henry to meet Francis I at Calais. After a secret marriage ceremony, which probably took place in Dover on 14 November, Henry and Anne were able to enjoy marital relations since the legitimacy of any child was assured. She had held out for six years against the king; now married, Anne conceived almost immediately in December 1532.

An official, but low-key, marriage followed in London on 25 January 1533, and Anne appeared with Henry that Easter. Catherine, meanwhile, refused to attend a further hearing on 1 May. Henry persisted in saying that his conscience troubled him over his relationship with his brother's widow, although his many affairs and possible bigamy hardly seemed to bother him at all.

An unpopular new queen

Catherine's marriage was declared null and void on 23 May 1533, just in time for Anne's Coronation at

Did you know?

Anne was crowned with the Crown of Edward the Confessor, normally used only for a reigning monarch. Did this symbolise Henry's great love for her? Or, as she was pregnant, was it actually the long-awaited son who was being anointed?

Westminster on 1 June, proceeded by a magnificent waterborne procession to the Tower of London and a ceremonial entry into the City. There were large crowds but, as Eustace Chapuys, Imperial Ambassador 1529–36, noted, there was little enthusiasm from the crowds. Chapuys was antagonistic towards Anne, but there is no doubt that she was unpopular with the masses.

Birth of Princess Elizabeth

On 7 September 1533, a baby girl, Elizabeth, was born. Henry was disappointed, as demonstrated by the cancellation of some – but not all – of the planned celebrations. At least it showed that Anne was fertile and able to produce a healthy baby.

The first years of her marriage were probably the happiest for Anne. This situation was made secure by further legislation in 1533–34: the *Act in Restraint of Appeals* prevented anyone (especially Catherine of Aragon) from making an appeal to Rome, whilst the *Act of Supremacy* and the *Treasons Act* specified Henry as Head of the Church in England, with severe penalties for non-compliance (under which Sir Thomas More and Bishop John Fisher were both executed in 1535). The *Act of Succession* named Elizabeth as heir.

An extravagant lifestyle

Vast amounts were spent on Queen Anne's clothes and jewels, as well as extensive programmes of luxurious palace refurbishments, with Henry and Anne's initials often used as a motif. At this time, as shown on the portrait medallion of 1534, Anne adopted as her motto 'The Moost Happi', choosing a crowned falcon with a sceptre as her personal heraldic device. Music, dancing and courtly life continued and in summer 1534 Anne was again pregnant, with Henry once more looking forward to a son.

ABOVE: An artist's impression of the Coronation procession of Anne Boleyn to Westminster Abbey.

LEFT: A stained-glass depiction of Anne Boleyn's heraldic white falcon.
FAR LEFT: 'AH' (Anne and Henry) monogram at Hampton Court Palace.

Anne and the Reformation

I
t has sometimes been maintained that without Anne Boleyn the
Reformation might not have occurred, either due to her own interests
in religious reform or the fact that Henry saw a break with Rome as
the only way in which he could marry her and obtain a male heir. The
English Reformation cannot be attributed to Anne Boleyn, although she
undoubtedly played a significant role in the whole process. The religious
climate in England was inclined to reform, as well as the wish to curb the

ABOVE: Thomas
Cromwell by
Hans Holbein
the Younger.

power and wealth of the Church. Anticlerical feeling was increasing amongst the general masses. Hostility caused by dislike of the worldliness, idleness and ignorance of many of the clergy had been highlighted since Chaucer's *Canterbury Tales* in the 14th century.

Anne certainly assisted some writers and reformers, bringing their works to the attention of her husband, such as Tyndale's *Obedience of a Christian Man* with which Henry became familiar. Highly educated, intelligent and independent, Anne was able to think for herself and had her own ideas about controversies such as 'justification by faith', the sale of indulgences and the 'new learning', but eventually this contributed to her downfall.

Anne and Wolsey

Anne's dealings with Cardinal Wolsey were always delicate and, allegedly, she bore a grudge against him for having prevented her marriage to Henry Percy. She sometimes appeared supportive, writing him profuse letters of thanks for his support: '… when I am queen … you shall find me the gladdest woman in the world … you shall have my love unfeignedly throughout my life' – but later became angry at his lack of success in achieving the divorce, turning Henry even more against him. Anne played a part in the removal of the powerful and unpopular Wolsey, but Henry also realised that this man was being obstructive in his desire to break with Rome.

> *"I cannot comprehend, and the King still less, how your reverend Lordship misled us by so many fine promises about divorce … and how you could have done what you have in order to hinder the achieving of our wishes."*
>
> ATTRIBUTED TO ANNE IN A LETTER TO WOLSEY

Anne and Cromwell

After the fall of Wolsey, Henry promoted Thomas Cromwell to increasingly senior posts until, by 1534, he was effectively running the country as Henry's Chief Minister. In spite of initially having a shared interest in reform of the Church, Anne clashed with Cromwell over the proposed Dissolution of the Monasteries, aimed at vastly increasing the wealth of the Crown whilst destroying age-old monastic traditions in education and helping with the poor and sick. Cromwell was in favour of an Imperial alliance whereas Anne had always been more pro-French, and she was increasingly meddling in politics and diplomacy. Cromwell became determined to bring about her downfall.

Disappointment and Discontent

So how and why did it all go wrong for Anne? As the old adage puts it, 'marrying the mistress creates a vacancy'. Anne's flirtatiousness, independence, high-level thinking and argumentative temperament were attractive in a mistress but not so desirable in a wife, who was supposed to do as she was told. As a highly educated and cultivated noblewoman, with interests in politics and religion, Anne had been helpful to Henry, but her main duty was to produce a son. Sadly, a second pregnancy resulted in a miscarriage in July 1534.

Henry's unfaithfulness

Anne and Henry's relationship soured as the strains of the break with Rome and lack of a male heir took their toll. She had rebuked Henry in 1533 for flirting while she was pregnant with Elizabeth. But in 1534 Henry took a new mistress, Anne's cousin, Margaret 'Madge' Shelton.

The years of waiting for a son by Anne can only have heightened Henry's prior expectations. When anticipated results do not materialise, disappointment can be immense, leading to feelings of blame, resentment and rage – even violence – and Henry's failed attempts to ensure the stability of his dynasty were turning him slowly from a dashing but power-hungry womaniser into a brute. Having finally married the one he had loved so long, he had expected that all would now come right, but events were not happening as planned.

OPPOSITE: Copy of a lost portrait of Henry VIII by Hans Holbein the Younger.

BELOW: Portrait of a lady by Hans Holbein the Younger, inscribed 'Anna Bollein Queen'.

Henry's loyalty

With no male heir, and Princess Elizabeth only two years old in 1535, many looked to Henry's other daughter, the Catholic Mary, as his successor, which might well lead to further civil war or foreign invasion. A male heir remained crucial and Henry, now approaching 45, appeared to be re-thinking his situation.

He seemed at times to be discontent with Anne, but there is also evidence, as the expert historian on the Tudor period Professor Ives points out, that during 1535 their relationship still continued as before. The summer progress that year was a huge success with much merriment and celebration. Henry offered Princess Elizabeth for an imperial marriage alliance, and was still very defensive of Anne when she was criticised, or if people made jokes at her expense. In spite of some difficulties, the king and queen still seemed to be getting on reasonably well and by October 1535 Anne was pregnant for the third time.

Anna Bollein Queen.

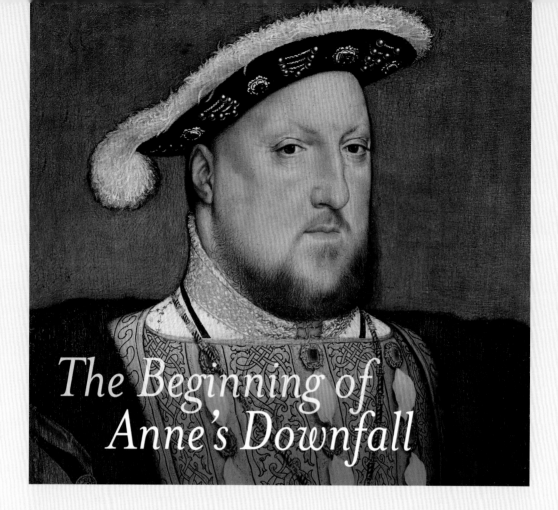

The Beginning of Anne's Downfall

ABOVE: Portrait of Henry by Hans Holbein the Younger, c.1537.

D ramatic events occurred rapidly in 1536 – the first on 7 January when Catherine of Aragon died, and Henry and Anne celebrated. Did Catherine's death make Anne feel more secure as queen – or worry that Henry could now repudiate his second marriage without running the risk of having to return to his first wife? Additionally, did Anne fear rejection if her latest pregnancy failed to provide Henry with a son?

Further disappointment

While jousting on 24 January, Henry had a serious brush with death, falling badly from his horse. After his accident, Anne miscarried, supposedly on the day of Catherine's funeral, 29 January. It was a male child of almost four months and it seemed that Anne had 'miscarried of her saviour'. However much Anne told Henry that the mishap was due to the shock of his accident, the king had now experienced a total of eight infant deaths or miscarriages, at least five of them boys. Historians have argued that the January miscarriage was the final straw and the point at which Henry and others determined that Anne had to go. But although the king was already

showing interest in Jane Seymour, other evidence suggests his relationship
with Anne was not yet doomed.

Developments of spring 1536

Anne, Henry and Elizabeth spent early spring 1536 together at Greenwich
Palace. May Day celebrations were planned, after which the king and queen
were to leave for Calais on 2 May. Extensive purchases of clothes, jewellery
and books were still being made for Anne, and grants of property and land
had been given to her, her father and her brother in March.

Cromwell quarrelled increasingly with Anne; on 2 April, her priest,
John Skip, delivered a sermon about a king's evil counsellor, clearly aimed
against Cromwell. In mid-April, Henry rejected proposals for a Treaty with
Charles V, and Cromwell's situation became dangerous. However, relations
remained agreeable between Henry and Anne: on Easter Tuesday, 18 April,
he publicly endorsed her position as queen, and Ambassador Chapuys,
caught off guard, bowed to her, at last implying recognition of her status.

However, on 23 April, St George's Day, Henry passed over Anne's brother
for the award of the Garter in favour of Nicholas Carew, a supporter of the
Seymours, clearly indicating some displeasure; and on 24 April, Cromwell
was authorised to investigate charges against Anne. On 25 April, in another
mood swing, Henry wrote to the English Ambassador in Rome, referring to
'the likelihood and appearance that God will send us heirs male', and
describing Anne as his 'most beloved wife'.

However, at the very end of April 1536, Henry suddenly became so angry
with Anne that he turned fiercely against her. Could it be that it was then
that Cromwell whispered in Henry's ear that he had evidence of Anne's
adultery? Henry would have been furious to have been cuckolded, but court
gossip was exactly what Cromwell needed.

Adultery and Treason

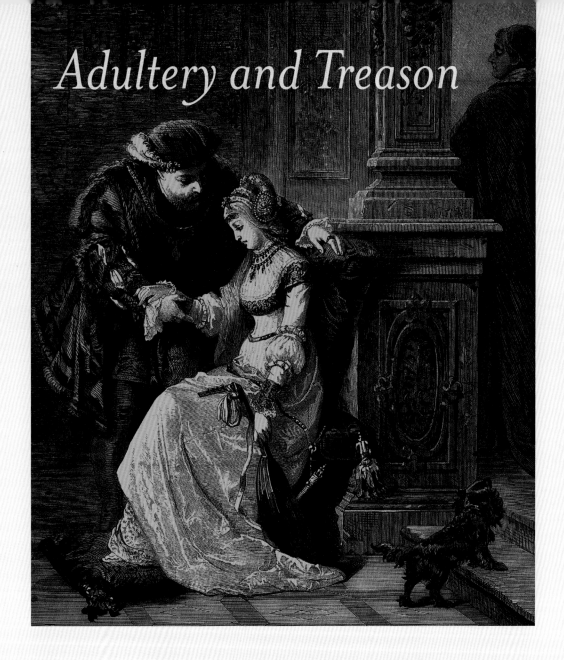

The last weekend of April 1536 proved fateful for Anne.

Overheard remarks

On Saturday 29 April, court musician Mark Smeaton was overheard expressing his devotion to Anne which she rejected. The following day, Anne was overheard joking with Sir Henry Norris that he must be looking to marry her if anything happened to the king. Wishing the king's death was treason: Norris was horrified and Anne rushed to Henry with Princess Elizabeth in her arms, declaring her love for the king and that it had just been banter. Unfortunately, Cromwell found out and on 30 April had Smeaton arrested and interrogated. Either because of torture, or perhaps because he was promised a pardon if he confessed, the musician admitted adultery with the queen. The May Day celebrations were to proceed but the trip to Calais planned for 2 May was cancelled at 11 p.m. on Sunday 30 April.

Cromwell's 'proof'

Cromwell had decided that Anne was a major threat and accusations of adultery would effectively remove her and her followers at the same time. The precipitating factor was probably not the loss of another boy, or because Henry had taken a fancy to Jane Seymour. The king's wrath, more likely, was that Cromwell now had 'proof' that Anne was unfaithful. The egotistical Henry had tired of Anne and was quickly convinced over that fateful weekend that she had made a fool of him. Between the 25 April letter to Rome and the 30 April arrest of Smeaton and the cancelled trip to Calais, the die was cast. Anne had to go.

ABOVE: Portrait of Thomas Cranmer, Anne's confessor, by Gerlach Flicke.

Further accusations

With Henry's approval, Cromwell investigated Anne on charges of adultery, treason and plotting the king's death. Perhaps Henry hoped Anne would go quietly, but to retain his own power and position Cromwell sought to get rid of her in a more final way. Annulment would clearly take too long but adultery could be regarded as treasonable since it threw into doubt the paternity of any son and heir. The May Day entertainment went ahead and Anne attended, throwing a handkerchief to a so-called 'lover' to mop his brow. But the celebrations were cut short; Henry left abruptly, riding back to York Place with Norris. He never saw Anne again.

Smeaton's confession on 1 May incriminated several high-ranking courtiers of the Privy Chamber. Anne's brother George (Viscount Rochford), Sir Henry Norris, Sir Francis Weston and William Brereton were all sent to the Tower of London. Further arrests of Sir Richard Page, poet Sir Thomas Wyatt and Sir Francis Bryan brought the total accused to eight. All except Smeaton maintained their innocence. They refused to admit to charges of adultery or treason although, unlike Smeaton, they were probably not tortured.

"'Master Kingston – shall I die without justice?' asked Anne, to which he replied, 'The poorest subject the King hath had justice,' whereupon she laughed."

As related by Cavendish in his *History of Wolsey*, 1558.

Arrest and Trials

R eceived at the Tower by Constable William Kingston on 2 May, Anne expressed surprise that she was in pleasant apartments rather than the dungeons. 'It is too good for me,' she said, relieved – a comment later held to be a confession of her guilt. She babbled continuously whilst imprisoned, and alternately wept or laughed hysterically. She was interrogated harshly by the Duke of Norfolk (her mother's brother) as she recounted her innocence in the incidents with Smeaton and Norris, adding a similar anecdote about Weston. These desperate attempts to explain her situation were used in Court; Anne was unwittingly supplying evidence against herself.

ABOVE: *Anne in the Tower* by Edouard Cibot.

Charges and the charged

Anne showed concern for her co-accused, especially her brother George, additionally accused of incest. She wrote a last letter to Henry on 6 May 1536, more a request for a fair trial than a declaration of love and fidelity. Page, Wyatt and Bryan were released but the trials of Smeaton, Norris, Weston and Brereton, charged with adultery, high treason and plotting the king's death, took place at Westminster on 12 May. It may seem odd that Henry made public his cuckolding, but he needed to blame Anne for all his misfortunes.

The evidence presented to the jury – packed with men hostile to Anne – was flimsy, since the dates of the alleged liaisons were largely impossible due to her presence elsewhere. Even Chapuys said the men were 'condemned by presumption'. All were found guilty and sentenced to death.

Anne's trial

Anne and George were tried on 15 May by a panel of peers headed by her uncle the Duke of Norfolk. Her father and Henry Percy were also present. Anne's trial was nonsensical since the accused men had already been convicted of adultery with her, and her alleged crimes were largely based on Smeaton's confession, court gossip, the libertine reputations of the men and her own unguarded remarks.

Anne was charged with adultery, incest, treason and plotting the king's death with a view to marrying one of her lovers. No transcript of the trial has survived and there was no legal defender. Scant evidence included Jane Rochford (George Boleyn's estranged wife) relaying comments by Anne about Henry's lack of sexual prowess and confirming George's overfamiliarity with his sister. Others reported that all the alleged 'bawdery and lechery' was too much to be believed.

Anne behaved in a brave and queenly manner, pleaded not guilty and gave a spirited defence. Even the hostile Chapuys recorded, 'These things she totally denied. And gave a plausible answer to each.' But the verdict was 'guilty'.

Anne's penalty was to be 'burned or beheaded … at the King's pleasure'. She remained calm, saying, 'Thou who art the way, the truth, and the life, knoweth whether I have deserved this … I have ever been a faithful wife to the King.'

Did you know?

Contrary to popular belief, no formal accusations of witchcraft were made against Anne.

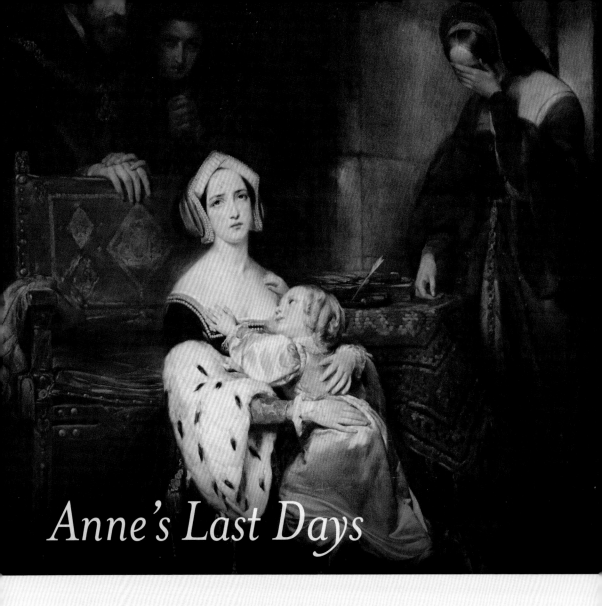

Anne's Last Days

After Anne was found guilty, her brother George was tried and spoke so well in his defence that most present were sure he would be acquitted. However, since his sister had been convicted of incest, there was no way he could escape and he too was found guilty.

Cranmer was to act as Anne's confessor and visited her in the Tower the next day, 16 May. He reported to Henry, 'I never had better opinion in a woman, than I did in her, which maketh me to think that she could not be culpable. And again, I think your Highness would not have gone so far, except that she had surely been culpable.'

Cranmer declared Anne and Henry's marriage annulled, probably to ensure there was no impediment to Henry's remarriage and the legitimacy of any future child – making Elizabeth illegitimate and eliminating her

ABOVE: Anne and Elizabeth by Gustaf Wappers.

from the succession. It is possible that Anne agreed to the annulment in the hope of a reprieve or perhaps an easier death. How could she be guilty of adultery, and hence treason, if she had technically never been married? Perhaps a bargain was struck, because the same day it was agreed that she could be beheaded, rather than burned.

Courageous to the end

The men were executed on 17 May and Anne prepared for her own execution two days later, famously observing 'I have a little neck', after which she burst out laughing. She may have still hoped for a miraculous last-minute reprieve from the man who had once loved her so dearly, but Henry's only friendly gesture was to employ an expert swordsman from France to ensure that her despatch was as quick as possible. Anne summoned Kingston to witness her swearing on her last sacrament that she was innocent; he later said that Anne 'seemed to have joy and pleasure in death'. Chapuys commented, 'No one ever showed more courage or greater readiness to meet death than she did.'

Anne went to her death dressed in royal robes trimmed with ermine, with a traditional gabled headdress, rather than the less demure French hood that had contributed both to her rise – and fall. She briefly addressed those present, then, blindfolded and kneeling upright, became confused as the executioner quickly swung his massive sword. Her body was buried swiftly in the chapel within the Tower of London.

It was just 1,000 days since she first dined as queen on Easter Sunday 1533; and only a month from when she was saluted as queen at Easter 1536 to the day of her execution, 19 May.

ABOVE: Anne's coat of arms, carved into the wall of the Beauchamp Tower in the Tower of London.

BELOW: Anne's final resting place: the Chapel Royal of St Peter ad Vincula at the Tower of London.

Did you know?

Rather than making a strong protestation of her innocence at her execution, Anne did what she could to protect Elizabeth and spoke well of Henry: 'I pray God save the king ... for a gentler nor a more merciful prince was there never: and to me he was ever a good, a gentle and sovereign lord.'

Guilty or Doomed?

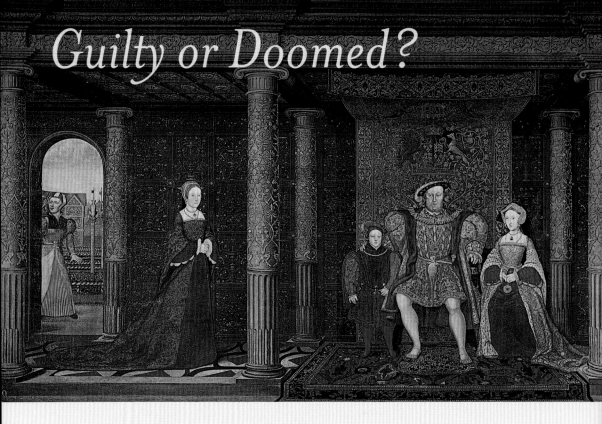

ABOVE: *The Family of Henry VIII* by an unknown artist, c.1545.

ABOVE: *The Family of Henry VIII* by an unknown artist, c.1545.

I t took seven years for Henry to dispose of his first wife; for the second less than seven weeks. Anne's trial might have been considered fair by the standards of the day, and although it appeared hasty and unjust it does not necessarily mean she was innocent. But it seems beyond belief that, after all her efforts to become a crowned queen, she would have risked everything for so little, or have been stupid enough to throw it all away for meaningless affairs.

"She made so wise and discreet answers to all things laid against her, excusing herself with her words so clearly as though she had never been faulty to the same."

CHRONICLER CHARLES WRIOTHESLEY OBSERVING ANNE BOLEYN'S TRIAL

Reasons ... or a foregone conclusion?

The only possible reason for adultery might be that Anne had concluded that her only chance to produce a male heir and save herself was to ensure she became pregnant by another man. This too seems unlikely. Perhaps, quite simply, she felt justified in seeking lovers to retaliate against the double standards of Henry.

And why should she have conspired to kill the king? What good would it have done her, unless she had simply come to dislike him so much? Henry's death would likely have resulted in her expulsion from the royal court and the recognition of his daughter Mary or some other claimant to the throne – not Anne's daughter Elizabeth with her as regent.

It seems somewhat irrelevant whether Anne was guilty or not. She swore on the sacrament, before witnesses and at the peril of her immortal soul that she was innocent; but Cromwell was casting about for legal reasons to put her to death and the verdict was a foregone conclusion.

Aftermath of Anne's death

Henry married Jane Seymour on 30 May, his second wife barely cold in her grave. Despite this, Anne's bright and intelligent daughter Elizabeth was eventually restored to the succession and became queen.

Within a few years of Anne Boleyn's beheading, all of her key opponents were dead, having died painfully or been executed. Henry – bloated, overweight and suffering terribly from leg ulcers, boils and gout – died in 1547. Cromwell, Cranmer and Jane Rochford were all eventually executed and it was only Henry's death that saved the Duke of Norfolk from meeting the same fate.

Was Anne guilty or just too flirtatious and indiscreet for her own good? Most experts consider that Anne and her co-accused were innocent of charges fabricated by Cromwell. Her real crime was not producing a son, for which she was arrested, tried, condemned and executed in the space of 17 days.

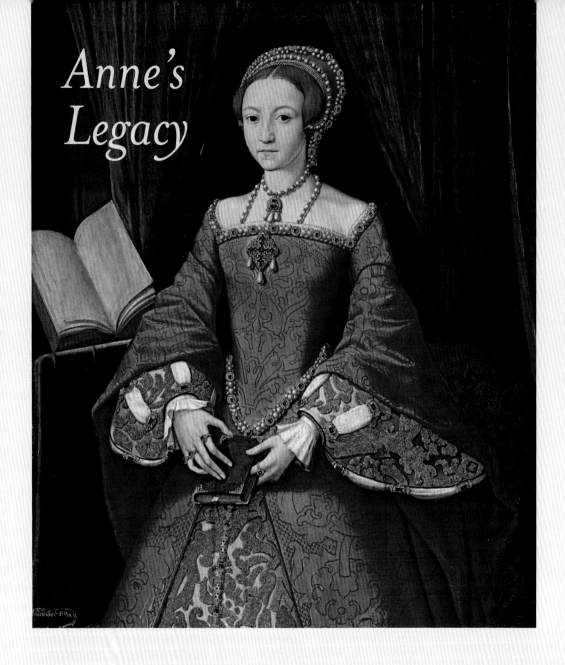

Anne's Legacy

ABOVE: Portrait of Princess Elizabeth, aged about 13.

A nne's legacy is much more important than the gruesome story of her death. She influenced the course of English and European history simply by virtue of Henry VIII falling in love with her, and because she gave birth to the monarch who made England a powerful force in the world from the late 16th century onwards.

Princess Elizabeth

Most members of the nobility had little daily contact with their children, but Anne had some influence during her daughter's formative years. From three months old Elizabeth lived separately at the palace at Hatfield, not seeing much of her mother, although receiving visits and gifts. However, from the age of seven months the princess lived near her parents, at Eltham, where they frequently visited her. She was at the court with them for much of 1535 and 1536, up to her mother's arrest. Elizabeth's loss of her mother (the circumstances becoming clear to her as she grew older) would have had a profound effect on her; perhaps it is no surprise that she did not marry, when her father had executed her mother.

Anne was fiercely protective of Elizabeth's rights and inheritance. She asked her chaplain, Matthew Parker (later Archbishop of Canterbury), to watch over the child, and ensured that she would be well-educated, guided by senior theologians and academics with interests in humanism and reform, such as John Cheke, Roger Ascham, William Cecil and John Dee – who all supported Elizabeth after she became queen in 1558.

Elizabeth carried her mother's memory with her in the form of a ring that she had made, containing their joint portraits, and also showed her devotion by her use of Anne's personal heraldic device: a falcon.

BELOW: Locket ring belonging to Elizabeth I, featuring miniature portraits of Elizabeth and her mother, Anne.

Anne's influence

Much discussion has taken place about the extent to which Anne influenced Henry VIII in religious, political and economic policies. Whilst it seems unlikely that without Anne the English Reformation might not have happened, she clearly made a significant contribution. Her charitable work was acknowledged by contemporaries; she undoubtedly helped the poor; and her love of the arts, fashion, music and dancing had a long-term effect.

Anne Boleyn is increasingly considered an early 'proto-feminist' heroine – educated, intelligent and able to stand up bravely to her male counterparts. Catholic writers like Nicholas Sander emphasised her wickedness, Protestants her charity and learning – and it is difficult to reconcile such opposing views.

Anne was unconventional and outspoken, and her appeal in the 21st century continues. Refusing to be submissive, she used her education, intelligence, spirit, courage and reasonably good looks to get what she wanted, even if her ambition eventually brought about her downfall.

Harlot or heroine, schemer or innocent victim … or something in between? We will never know for sure.